Indra's Net

Indra's Net

Dedicated to the gifted poets Cynthia Jobin and
Bart Wolffe, both of whom died while this volume was
being prepared for publication.

All profits from the sale of this anthology will go to The
Book Bus charity which aims to improve child literacy
rates in Africa, Asia and South America by providing
children with books and the inspiration to read them.
www.thebookbus.org

Huge thanks to all the poets featured in *Indra's Net* who so
generously donated outstanding examples of their work to
help raise funds for The Book Bus.

Cover design by Kristina Burgess, inspired by jali at the
Taj Mahal. The Hindi word 'jali' means 'net' or 'mesh'
and is used to refer to often highly ornamental window
screens based on calligraphic or geometric designs.
Thank you, Kristina.
www.kristinaburgess.co.uk

Copyright ©2017 Bennison Books
All rights reserved
First published 2017

This book is sold subject to the condition that it
shall not be reproduced in any form without the prior
written permission of Bennison Books. Brief quotations
may be used without permission
in articles or reviews.

Bennison Books Poetic Licence
978-1-9997408-0-1

bennisonbooks.com

Contents

Foreword by Carol Rumens 1

Edward Ahern 5

    Seasoning 6
    A Winter's Day 7
    The Snowstorm 8

Betty Hayes Albright 9

    Without Roots 10
    Points of Light 11

Veronica Aldous 12

    Woods 13
    What is it like to lie in the attic concealed with the
    covering of dust upon the dust cover? 15
    Oolie 16

Karin Andersen 17

    Waiting for You 18
    The End of the World 19
    Becoming Stillness 20

Paul Beech 21

    Scallywags 22

Beverley Bie Brahic..23

   White Sheets 24
   The Sleep of the Magi 26
   Vinegar and Salt 28

Glenda Kerney Brown 29

   The Box..30
   From the Other Side 31
   Green Lane 32

Salvatore Buttaci...33

   Sunny Side Up 34
   Only Those Who Are Stuffed With Straw.....................35

A Carder 36

   Nefertiti in Jeans 37
   The Floating Fleeting World................38
   Lacuna...39

Ethel Mortenson Davis...40

   A Day..41
   Cottontail..43
   The Dance...44

Thomas Davis...46

   "By God, They're Protecting Salamanders Instead of
   Human Beings".....................................47
   Peach Cobbler, the Beautiful Baker's Song 48

DM Denton 50

   An Artist Revealed...............................51
   Stolen Fruit 52

Alyson Faye...53

    Very Like Vermeer..54
    Rooks' Flight...55
    The Poppy Parade...57

Bruce Goodman..58

    Bury Me Flamboyantly Clad..59
    It's Pretty..60

Helen Harrison..62

    Mum and Spuds...63
    The Rhythm of Wood...64

Judith Highcock..65

    Mount Pisgah...66
    Mid-Winter Landscape..67
    The Beach...68

Cynthia Jobin...69

    The Sun Also Sets...70
    Ode to a Condiment..71
    Getting It..72

Marianne Jones...74

    Spring Cleaning..75
    The Romantic...76

Vanessa Kirkpatrick..77

    Apple..78
    Wittstock, 1946..80
    Leaving...83

Jim Kleinhenz 85

Milk by Morning 86
Pavane Pour une Infante Défunte 87

Elizabeth Leaper 88

About Morning 89
Old Photographs 91
Lambing 93

John Looker 95

Newborn 96
The Perfectionist 97
The Escape to Troy 98
And to a Winter's Day Also … 100

A.J. Mark 101

Angel in the Snow 102
The Timbre of Frost 103
Lanterns 104

Frédéric G. Martin 105

Between Chatou and Croissy 106
Forgotten Sandcastles 107

Chris McLoughlin 108

Pijaykin 109

Chris Moran 111

Dad's Hat 112
Past Lives 113
Crying Over Spilt Tea 114

Anna Mosca 116

   Stories Within Lines 117
   No Hands 118
   Beautiful Beauty 120

Robert Okaji 121

   How to Write a Poem 122
   Hail 124
   Arthritis 125

Jim Winton Porter 126

   Biology 127
   Winged Crosses 128
   Two Nights 129

Jean Rodenbough 131

   Water 132
   After Snow 133
   As Nature is to God as Child, so is Art to Nature 134

Martin Shone 135

   A Moment of Snowfall 136
   Sharp Echoes 137
   Sunrise 138

Ina Schroders-Zeeders 139

   The Balance 140

Lauren Scott 141

   One Kiss 142

Katharine Towers 143

    Double Concerto 144
    The Window 145
    The Way We Go 146

Rob Walton 147

    An Alien Complains 148
    The Thing About the Words 150

Maureen Weldon 152

    Midnight Robin 153
    He Tells Her 154
    The Past 155

Frederick E. Whitehead 156

    Grind 157
    Steerage 159

Sarah Whiteley 160

    Ciphers 161
    At Talapus 162
    The Peony 163

Jane Williams 164

    I have Come to Believe 165

Sandy Wilson 166

    The Arc of Time 167
    The Caress of Spring 168

Bart Wolffe...169

    The Boy Who Never Grew Up 170
    Tinker, Tailor Soldier, Sailor 171
    Eclipse...172

The Book Bus...174

Fulfilment

I had a hope – for truth and explanation.
I had a friend – who leaves no name, no trace.
I had a mind, and wore it on my face
Exposed to time and sunlight's slow cremation.
Where are those blinding sight-spots? In a place
I can go back to? No, the children said,
They're waiting for you. Look, just up ahead.

Carol Rumens, Blind Spots (Seren, 2008)

Postcard for the Youngest Child

Your sky, my sky
share the same
smoke-drifts, pearls,
feathers of snow.

My years stream
their weather. Yours
are bare new hills.

Climb. Climb slow.

Carol Rumens, Animal People (Seren, 2016)

Foreword
By Carol Rumens

Indra is a Vedic god, above whose mountain-palace hangs a marvellous net. Sparkling at every point where the threads intersect is a multi-facetted jewel. Each jewel reflects every other jewel.

The title of this anthology, *Indra's Net*, was suggested by one of its poets, the late Cynthia Jobin. She explained: "Indra's net is a metaphor for universal interconnectedness. It's as old as ancient Sanskrit and as 'today' as speculative scientific cosmology. It's what came to mind when thinking about nets and webs and interconnectedness … and jewels and poems."

There are many ways in which the metaphor suits the anthology. It's a book filled with poetic gems, of course, the work of a happy mixture of new and well-known writers, including prizewinning poets like Beverley Bie Brahic and Katharine Towers. The poems connect: poems always do. The poets may have shared their work and reached their global readership via the Internet. And then there's the most important net of all, described by Wallace Stevens as "The magnificent cause of being,/ The imagination, the one reality/ In this imagined world …"

The Book Bus itself may be seen as an extension of the

metaphor, as a transporter and sharer of the jewelled net of literacy.

About forty poets from many different countries around the world have donated poems to this anthology. All profits will help The Book Bus, which carries not only books, libraries and reading programmes but immeasurable opportunity to children across Africa, Asia and South America.

Like all poems, these are about individual thoughts and feelings, and about language itself. Poems are as personal as DNA. And in every language and dialect on earth, poetry is one of the peaks of that community's identity. Its rhythms shape memory and knowledge. It enhances and sharpens both the ordinary and the more unusual events and emotions which form us and our lives.

Readers will enjoy this varied and accessible anthology, and have the added satisfaction of knowing their purchase is helping to hand on the pleasure and power of language. They will have added another small jewel to Indra's net.

Carol Rumens, 2017.

Carol Rumens's latest collections of poetry are *Perhaps Bag* (Sheep Meadow, 2017) and *Animal People* (Seren, 2016). A Fellow of the Royal Society of Literature, she has published short stories, a novel (*Plato Park*, Chatto, 1988), a trio of poetry lectures, *Self into Song* (Bloodaxe, 2007) and occasional translations of Russian poetry with her late partner, Yuri Drobyshev. She teaches Creative Writing at

Bangor University, Gwynedd, and contributes a popular weekly blog, "Poem of the Week", to *The Guardian Books Online*. She has received the Cholmondeley Award and the Prudence Farmer Prize, and was joint recipient of an Alice Hunt Bartlett Award.

~4~

Edward Ahern

Ed Ahern resumed writing after forty-odd years in foreign intelligence and international sales. He has his original wife, but advises that after forty-nine years they're both out of warranty. He works the other side of writing at Bewildering Stories, where he sits on the review board and manages a posse of five review editors.

Ed's had 140 stories and poems published to date, and a series of articles on fly fishing. His collected fairy and folk tales *The Witch Made Me Do It* was published by Gypsy Shadow Press. His novella *The Witches' Bane* was published by World Castle Publishing, and his collection of fantasy and horror stories *Capricious Visions* was published by Gnome On Pig Productions.

Ed's currently working on a paranormal/thriller novel tentatively titled *The Rule of Chaos*. He lives in Fairfield, Connecticut, USA.

Seasoning

Over the years
Several women drew close,
Differing in marvellous ways.
But all, early on or later in the time together,
Were pushed away or saw enough to leave.
Remembered in swirls of abiding fondness.
Piquant almosts sprinkled on a bland existence.

A Winter's Day

When snow's gone dead with cold
And makes a brittle crunch
When air's a choking slush
That sears the lungs to suck
When fingers touch a frozen mouth
That cannot speak of feeling
Then winter's squatted frigidly
On all the open ground
And driven off with frost-bit whips
All those who live by warmth
Yet thought they owned the world.

The Snowstorm

The wind shoves the flakes downward,
a falling, frozen cloud that seals
the man-made lawns and walks
beneath howling, formless anarchy.

The road unploughed, the car buried,
poor-me chatter bouncing across the screen.
There is little that would induce me
to burrow out and slew my way from home.

Loss of power, truly close friend, hunger.
My world, after all, is small.

Betty Hayes Albright

Betty lives in the northwest corner of the United States with her husband, David. She has been writing poetry since the age of ten.

Her previous publications include a chapbook, *Living Color*, and an ebook, *Runes*. She has also been published in a variety of small magazines and newspapers.

In the mid 1990s she enjoyed being a member of The Seattle Live Poets which gave readings throughout the Seattle area.

Betty's poetry blog, 'Seasonings', can be found at http://raindancepoetry.wordpress.com

Without Roots

South winds
push the great tree
to mortal degree,
its many arms thrashing
in dark circles,
its body twisted in deep groan;
and I would be that bird
perched white at the top.
I'd play the storm
swaying in brave arcs
without roots.

Points of Light

Poetry is the well-worn sleeve
where she displays her heart.
Somebody said
the gods wear paisley,
angels dip their toes
in velvet pleats,
but she likes best
a weave of silk
with lace crochet
around the edge.
Look closely
at the points of light
between the threads,
you'll see his face
and maybe even read his name
embroidered coyly
near her wrist.
Day after day
she sews anew
the fragile seams
that join her dreams
all neatly hemmed
and pressed –
or so it seems.

Veronica Aldous

Veronica is an artist and poet. She has written three poetry and short story collections and is on the way to publishing her fourth. *Mortal* and *Moon Cinema* were edited by the late great Bart Wolffe. All are available on Amazon and Lulu.

Veronica lectures in Creative Writing and Fine Art for Reigate School of Art. Her writing is inspired by a strong engagement with nature and a powerful imagination informed by the magic realist movement. The sound and shape of words are textures which thread in and out of her work. She believes poetry lies on the border of perception and memory and is a way of fruitfully replaying intense experience.

Veronica was brought up in the Hertfordshire countryside (UK) and being sensually and emotionally connected with the landscape and with nature is an abiding theme. A sense of humour and of Eros interplay with more serious themes of mortality, memory and places. Her work has been described as rich as a populous plum pudding, full of visceral imagery, delicious alliteration and studded with her fine vocabulary.

Veronica's popular poetry blog can be found at www.veronicaaldous.wordpress.com

Woods

They say the higher trees know more of stillness
The woods respire, they feel the sun in an open senseless way
They do not require our words, but feed
On worm mould, imbibing with the tentacles of arterial animalic
Tubes, quick fired leaf-turbines, protuberances which bulge
Prolapsed and hard as whalebone, like ailments which are
      talismanic
And to be desired, lacunae which ossify and howl in high winds
Sinuses full of peppered moth and ropey larvae and kittenish
      owls
Interstices of pulp, honey fungus, obscene saddles, priapic herms
Things to piss on, mount and squirm on, throttling ivy, old man's
      beard,
A virgin's answer to her panhandling experimental prayers
No wonder we think them inhabited by hamadryads
No wonder we venerate them, curse them for the heavy leaf fall
Like yards and yards of fabric stitched by veinous liney threads
Useless clotting cloth, only good for burning, blowing into bags
To rot into uncultured humus, greedy things that swallow
      themselves
Heaving up like tumuli they embed the sky with a myriad lysergic
      replications
Fractals of life itself, inward turning, evolving rays and eyes
Forever moving dirty core into the outer derma
Oh you can stare
At spinneys till you fall down under them
Buried in ecstatic lack of understanding

For why we are here
Under such indifferent, churning skies.

What is it like to lie in the attic concealed with the covering of dust upon the dust cover?

I'll tell you: the nights come one on one the little stars rise
their eyes alight on the whitening shape
of me up there with the spiders and the carcases of moths
but I'm quite happy with my lucubrations, my stump of candle
the scratchy pen, the torn up cloth I use for writing, drawing
you won't see my art – it's all invisible, except the scrap
I'm working on, it takes me years to get the details right
but line on line and word on word the pieces come together
I'm making it slowly, there's cosmology in my fingers
the stiller I lie and the smaller my movements –
the better the outcome
if you come up those wooden stairs, you won't find me there
I am not discernible , I am wrapped in shrouds, I'm ectoplasm
shadows of shadows and beetles on the window pane
you'd think I was a worn out chair –
I 'm up here waiting for moulds to erupt into flower
the cracks in the walls to whisper some secrets
I've got so little and I only want you
and you're so slow coming, I wish you were here
sometimes I whine and whimper because I love you
that's quite annoying –
especially for the visitors who are downstairs
sometimes I sing and that's much better
then they knock upon the ceiling
shout 'shut up, shut up! – o you noisy crow!'

Oolie

Knit in chain mail brown wool, saved from some workman's
         jumper,
Oolie was a felted bird with plastic pre-war eyes
A joyless thing which never mattered much and therefore stays
Rooted in the memory like some symbol which has gone unread
He smelled stale and sweaty like a three-week unmade bed.

They had no yellow left and made a beak of green, his ear tufts
Rudimentary dog-eared stitching, he was rough and itchy
To the kiss, what child could be comforted by such rectangular
Brutality, or nestle in his permanent frozen glassy stare?
Who made him, gifted him, loved him? I only know the last.

A hair shirt of a toy .Yet he too was loved
Despite his faults; dropped stitches and unloveliness –

And I forgive the boy.

Karin Andersen

Born in Zimbabwe, Karin has also lived in France, England and Tunisia. She currently calls Cape Town home, but will soon be moving to a small country village, where she hopes to grow both vegetables and poems.

Karin has had poems published in two of the annual Sol Plaatjie anthologies, in a collective work called *A Woman sits down to write* and *The Wagon*, a literary journal published monthly in India. Her work was also included in the anthology *Writing the Self*. She blogs at http://sometimesilove.wordpress.com

Waiting for You

I drove down the midnight highway
the road lit with pools of orange light,
a night watchman shadow-boxing behind a fence,
me, smoking, choking on desire.

The arrival board blinked
Air France ETA 01.20.
Legs shaking I sat,
my hands clenched between my knees.
A scattering of people slouched around me.

The doors slid open, feet shuffled,wheels rattled.
I stood on tiptoe,
My breath so high in my chest
that it almost vanished.
I looked for you,
your sharp beak of a nose, your wiry strength,
your blond hair,
my gold earring in your ear, yours in mine.

The conveyor belt emptied, sighed to a halt.
The lights dimmed,
leaving me, a porter, a cleaner with a mop.
The flight crew came through last.
No one else.
I drove home.
There was no moon that night.

The End of the World

All my life I've dreamed of the apocalypse.
When I was a child I barred the doors
and windows against the invasions
that came when I slept.

Now that I'm grown
I still dream that it's coming
I pack a bag and flee,
home is no longer a refuge.

When I'm awake I believe it will come
in slow small steps, unnoticed,
until it's too late to get away.

Today I saw it
in the bodies of children
sleeping in the forest,
sprawled in town squares
on the other side of the world.

Then I turned and looked and knew
that it's been here
all the time
behind me.

Becoming Stillness

I'm watching your skin
fold and drape
with tired yellow elegance
across your bones.
The bowl of your hips
lies empty on the bed.
Your hands hold no pen, no brush
your sketch pad is closed.

The morphine
winding sluggish
through your veins
is the only sound I hear.
I hold your wrist,
listen with my fingers.

Paul Beech

Paul Beech is a Lancashire lad now living in North Wales. He writes poetry, flash fiction and stories for children. His work has been published in various magazines, journals and anthologies and he enjoys reading at poetry events. His first collection, *Twin Dakotas: poetry and prose,* was published by Cestrian Press in 2016.

Paul is a retired social housing manager whose specialisms included sheltered housing and helping the homeless. He is a member of Chester Poets and Cross-Border Poets (Mold, UK).

More of his work can be found online at Grandy's Landing: http://paulbeech.wordpress.com.

Scallywags

Nice morning, soft blue,
cheeky beaks at my window;
the sparrows are back.

Chirpy scallywags
gossiping in the laurel;
quick wings beat the air.

Nice morning, soft blue,
I feel like a boy again.
Aye, the sparrows are back.

Beverley Bie Brahic

Beverley Bie Brahic is a poet and translator. A Canadian, she lives in Paris and the San Francisco Bay Area in the United States of America. Her second poetry collection, *White Sheets*, was a finalist for the 2012 Forward Prize.

Her translations include *Guillaume Apollinaire, The Little Auto*, winner of the 2013 Scott Moncrieff Prize; *Francis Ponge, Unfinished Ode to Mud*, a finalist for the 2009 Popescu Prize for Poetry in Translation; Yves Bonnefoy's *The Present Hour, Rue Traversière,* and *The Anchor's Long Chain;* and books by Jacques Derrida, Julia Kristeva *(This Incredible Need to Believe*, a finalist for the 2010 French-American Foundation Translation Prize) and Hélène Cixous, including *Portrait of Jacques Derrida as a Young Jewish Saint,* and *Manhattan.*

Her most recent poetry collection, *Hunting the Boar*, is a 2016 Poetry Book Society Recommendation.

White Sheets

Airstrike hits wedding party – breaking news

The empty laundry basket
fills with molecules of light.
She stands beside it, arms falling
into the aftermath of the task.
Gesture is a proto-language
researchers say: the same circuits
light the brain when a chimp
signals *help me please* (hand
outstretched, palm up) as when
human beings process speech.
In the cave the hunter figure
mirrors his spear's trajectory
towards the deer it will never,
of course, attain. The woman
sees nothing untoward. Her body
bars the spattered something
in the middle distance, though all
of this is right up close: the shed
they'll use to dress the meat, the plane
geometry of white sheets
on a line. The world is beautiful,
she thinks, or feels, as deer
sense something coming
and move out of range. Beautiful,

the woman thinks, and lifts
the laundry basket to her arms –
beautiful, and orderly.

From *White Sheets*, CB editions, 2012.

The Sleep of the Magi

Gislebertus hoc fecit

They bivouack in Autun Cathedral.
The sculptor draws a sheet
around them, wrinkled as a pond

when a stone skips and
shock rings expand,
fraying a little. Three heads on one pillow:

they've kept their crowns —
how could we know them
without their crowns?

. . .

One stares into the dark.
Doesn't see the Angel
standing behind, index finger
wagging at the star

that looks like a flower.
It went behind a cloud
and they lay down
to wait for it to clear up, so tired

of journeying that Gabriel,
whose wings are like the fish-scale tile

of a Burgundy mansion,
has come to wake them.

From *Hunting the Boar*, CB editions, 2016.

Vinegar and Salt

Here is the bench where we can sit
and watch the waves go in and out.
Lean back, sop up the horizontal sun
trawling west across the Strait.
Why don't I leave you here? you say,
why don't I take a walk out where
the tide will turn, that wave-stamped
swathe of darker, wetter sand

where families shore up their castle walls
and sift debris for intact shells,
faux gems of bottle glass, and fossil scraps
of runic, worm-written wood
the sea collects for us to hold.
And while I'm at it, why don't I stop —
pick us up some fish and chips
at last summer's take-out stand?

Glenda Kerney Brown

Glenda grew up in Baildon, a small West Yorkshire village in the UK. She studied Drama and English at Swansea University but her ambition to pursue an acting career was thwarted by a diagnosis of multiple sclerosis. As a result, Glenda confesses that she 'stumbled' into poetry instead.

Now a wheelchair user, Glenda writes her poetry using an interactive voice program. She originally wrote poems for children which she performed at primary schools, but after joining a local writing class led by the Yorkshire poet James Nash, Glenda began writing poetry for adults.

She lives with her husband who is also her full-time carer, but refuses to describe her situation as grim in any way. Writing poetry, says Glenda, defines who she is and she loses herself for hours in her work, re-emerging 'physically tired but mentally invigorated'.

Her poetry collection, *Rock and Lodestone*, was published by Bennison Books in 2016.

The Box

The box is black, olden, Eastern,
bearing swaddled symbols,
embers of fire in the memory:
kin koi carp in mid-leap, lunging,
lilies leaning, pinned with butterflies,
and butterflies, butterflies, lifting
the mottled green leaves, which trail
direct from the islands of Japan.

*Kin is a Japanese word pertaining specifically to
koi carp, meaning golden metallic.*

From the Other Side

You chose to go, and I wonder
if your implacable decision forming
fundamentals were imperfect,
when you tiptoed, whirled, strode
or thundered to your assignation
with your under-polished oven
and its ruthless breath.
Does your vibrant spirit sometimes
wander to the great wall to watch
us doing dishes, splashing ephemeral
bubbles born to die, gorging ourselves
on sensation, and do you feel desire?

Green Lane

The market's quilted cobblestones feast the eyes,
bounce your bottom like a tennis ball as you make
for Mr Magic who can fix your broken purse.

Inaccessible pubs overflow cosy with gnarled, nicotine
leaky beams: dad would sniff his bloodhound's way
to every bar, polish it over riotous years with patched

elbow and bonhomie, drunks hoisting his skinny frame
in the chair, shoulder high over steps, if he were you,
and not dead. You plunder imagination from desire.

Green Lane nibbles the Chevin's heel, tipsy with
cowslips and feathery ferns. *All right, Bunny?*
he asks, loping the never was, never looking back.

Salvatore Buttaci

Salvatore Buttaci is a self-confessed obsessive-compulsive writer who plies his craft for hours each day. A former middle-school English teacher and a writing instructor at Bergen Community College in Parumus, New Jersey, in the United States, his poems, stories, letters and articles, have appeared widely in publications such as *The New York Times, Christian Science Monitor, Cats Magazine, The Writer, Writer's Digest,* and many others.

In 2007, he was the recipient of the $500 AZsacra International Poetry Award for his poem, 'Soldier Killed in Iraq'. He is the author of four poetry collections: *Promising the Moon; If Rosters Don't Crow, It Is Still Morning: Haiku and other Poems; A Dusting of Star Fall;* and *Two Can Play This Game…* (co-authored with Paul Juszcyk).

In addition, Salvatore is the author of two flash-fiction collections *Flashing My Shorts* and *200 Shorts,* both published by All Things That Matter Press and available at Amazon.com. His book *A Family of Sicilians,* which critics called 'the best book written about Sicilians' is available at Lulu.com.

Salvatore is now retired and lives in West Virginia with his wife Sharon, his love and inspiration.

Sunny Side Up

An eggshell dawn cracked across the heavens,
infusing morning clouds with new-day gold.
Rising early from sleep, storm-tossed from dreams,
we sip hot coffee on the back porch deck
and marvel at the rays of yellow high roads
streaking like gifting fingers from the sun.
How good it is to be alive, you say,
to once again witness God's Creation.
We are blessed. Coffees at rest, we hold hands
while high above us birds flock a halo
around the brow of the rising jewel.

Only Those Who Are Stuffed With Straw

They know how empty are the threats of crows,
how their frantic fluttering black wings conceal
the sun, their cawing streak around their heads
in search of button eyes to poke away.
Alone in the alfalfa fields, they stand
unmoving. Only their flannel shirts,
their coveralls, hats too made of straw
are nudged by playful winds that scurry
through the labyrinth of trembling leaves.

Just exactly what do they know, these straw
sentries? What do they care? What can they feel?
Farmer Gray mutters his profanities;
he shakes a calloused fist at the dark-bird sky.
But the straw man stands on neither side
of profit and gain, in the black, in the red.
Those stuffed with straw know the gift of sunshine
in which, without worry or distraction,
they bask in the comfort of its rays.

A Carder

A Carder is a pseudonym. 'Card' is a verb, meaning to comb, clean and disentangle raw wool to make it ready for spinning.

A Carder's collection of prose poems, *Between Dusk and Darkness*, published by Bennison Books, is available from Amazon.

Nefertiti in Jeans

Then, on the bus, you turned and kissed my left temple.
And the old men half-puckered and the women shining
above their shopping, and me Nefertiti in jeans.

The woman in the bakery folded our French stick in
half as if subduing a wrestler. And so began our
stockpile of private treasures. In such moments lives
are arranged, more final than a marriage. And every
bakery since, every inhalation of fresh-baked bread, a
reminder of that consecration.

You made curry, its exotic aroma narcotic, and
everything changed for all time.

The Floating Fleeting World

I pulled up my hair and you
leant forward to kiss the nape
of my neck. The memory is so
clear, so vivid, so outside of
time, that even now as I write
I lift my hand to touch the
spot where your mouth
pressed against my skin.

Lacuna

1911

The Mona Lisa, or La Gioconda, is stolen from the Salon Carré at the Louvre by Vincenzo Peruggia, an Italian workman.

The museum reopens a week later and people queue to stare at the sudden absence: the blank wall between Correggio's Mystic Marriage of Saint Catherine and Titian's Allegory of Alfonso d'Avalos.

One man leaves flowers.

The absence is more eloquent, more piercing. This is an exquisite region where it is possible to know; where an understanding can be glimpsed; where we can be outside ourselves.

I study the space you once filled. I trace the markings that you left, your bright shadow. As if the space is your quiddity, because gone, you are more here than ever. As if your leaving is your definition.

Always, there is loss: as unexpected and implausible as a miracle. A mystery of leaving.

I jostle in a queue of selves to *see*.

I come, I leave flowers, and a lachrymal vase.

You touch the core of me.

Ethel Mortenson Davis

Ethel Mortenson Davis has published three books of poetry, *I Sleep Between the Moons of New Mexico*, *White Ermine Across Her Shoulders*, and *The Healer*. She is currently working on a fourth book. Trained as an artist at the University of Wisconsin-Madison, her poetry is intensely visual, demonstrating the same life, colour, and movement as her pastels. It has appeared in anthologies, literary journals, and magazines. Her artwork has been shown in a number of galleries in Wisconsin and New Mexico and has appeared in various journals and magazines.

She is currently a resident of Sturgeon Bay, Wisconsin, on the Door County peninsula, one of the writing and art centres of the Midwest United States. She blogs at www.fourwindowspress.com with her husband, Thomas Davis, publishing poetry, artwork, photographs, and an occasional essay.

Born in Wausau, Wisconsin, her parents were dairy farmers. Her years on the farm instilled a deep sense of being part of the earth and animals, forests, water, and plant life. It is this sense of the interrelatedness of nature and human community that makes up the themes of her poetry.

A Day

It is a day
when the earth
turns just right,

when fish swim
close to the top
of the great lake
to feed on insects or plants,

when black-winged pelicans
dive in and out to fish,

and fishermen gather
in clumps, throwing
out their lines.

It is a day
before the storm,
humid and cloudy,

when the two of you
think of ways to
come together

as part
of a turning of the universe,

a love that blows
a sweetness over us –

something unexpected.

Cottontail

Crazy cottontail,
spinning in the desert,
running in circles
in snow
mixed with rain.

Must be happy,
back and forth.

Greening
of the world
means
eating again.

The Dance

At sunrise
she began to dance

so that humanness

would seep back
into the earth,
into the lowest
parts of the earth.

She danced for
the murdered,
and missing,
the lost and forsaken.

Then,
she danced
all through the night

for the inhumanness

that filled her heart,

for the hatred and lack of love
that had captured her.

She danced and danced
until inhumanity

drained out of her,
out of the farthest parts
of the earth,

until the sun
came back to the world.

Thomas Davis

Thomas Davis is the author of five published works, including his epic poem, *The Weirding, A Dragon Epic* published by Bennison Books and *Sustaining the Forest, the People, and the Spirit* by State University of New York (SUNY) Press, and three novels. He has also edited three magazines, and a poetry anthology, and had articles and essays published in a variety of magazines and journals. Two of his plays have been produced by small theatre groups.

In addition to his writing he has been the President or Chief Academic Officer of five tribal colleges or universities in the United States. The tribal college movement has helped spur a worldwide movement to develop indigenous controlled colleges supporting native cultures through higher education. He is also known for his work in helping to found the World Indigenous Higher Education Consortium (WINHEC) and advocating the use of Science, Technology, Engineering, and Math (STEM) education to generate economic development opportunities in poor communities.

Tom and his wife Ethel Mortenson Davis publish a blog of poetry, art and photography at www.fourwindowspress.com

"By God, They're Protecting Salamanders Instead of Human Beings"

An Italian sonnet

When Darwin saw gradation in a finch
That flits about Galapagos, he saw
One species modified in beak and claw
By choices made adapting to the flinch
Of circumstances born out of the wrench
Of geologic time, the pitch and yaw
Of land and ocean, weather systems raw
With winds that shape the land that rainstorms drench.

But in his old age earthworms sang the song
That sirened through the studies that he did,
The deaf and blind regurgitator dug
Into plain ground turned soil, the endless round
Of earth built by the living plows that slid
Fecundity out of the realm of slugs.

Peach Cobbler, the Beautiful Baker's Song

Unable to sleep, she got up at three
and went outside where silver moon horned night
below a star glittering and dancing in a twinkle.
She went over to the back yard's three peach trees
and waved her hand in darkness along branch bark
until she had picked a large, round peach from each tree.
Inside the kitchen the song the universe was singing
was a little off-key, as if her being up in the middle of night
was unkiltering the lining up of stars and moon.

She went to the cupboard, pulled out flour
ground from sunflowers and daisy essence
and peeled huge peaches
whose slices failed to fit into her largest bowl.
Smiling to herself in the moon's dim light,
she lit the old wood stove before rolling out peach cobbler
    crust,
mixing honey, nectar, and the sound of the flight of bees
into the rich, shining peach slices,
covering the cobbler with petals of red and yellow roses
picked the evening before from beside a dark pool
glimmering starshine and a faint trace of moon.
In the great cast-iron oven fire crackled and danced.
Bats flew from the attic to swoop crazily in the kitchen
as the woman wiped hands on her apron
and hummed a silver song that had no words,

but bubbled and popped into the cobbler's fillings
as cooking peach smells mixed with firewood smells
and woke a symphony of night, stars, sky, moon, and earth.

When the cobbler was done and out of the oven,
the wood fire stoked,
the woman took a deep breath and yawned.

"Maybe I can sleep now," she said.

She left the kitchen, climbed the stairs
to where her husband was snoring oblivion,
and closed her eyes as sun sent yellow fire
over hills and the day's horizon.

DM Denton

Author and artist Diane M Denton (nee DiGiacomo) is a native of Western New York in the United States.

Her educational journey included a dream-fulfilling semester at Wroxton College in England, where she then stayed for 16 years – a life-changing experience that continues to resonate in her personal and professional endeavours to this day.

She returned to America in 1990, to a rural area of Western New York State where she lives in a cosy log cabin with her eighty-something mother and a multitude of cats.

She has written two historical novels inspired by the real-life seventeenth century composer Alessandro Stradella, published by All Things That Matter Press: *A House Near Luccoli* and *To A Strange Somewhere Fled*.

Diane is currently working on a novel-length account of Anne Brontë's life. Visit her website and blog:
http://www.dmdenton-author-artist.com/
http://bardessdmdenton.wordpress.com/

An Artist Revealed

The secrets of your heart
are stacked against the wall,
canvases for your art
of hiding what you missed.
No mistaking your style,
a freedom out of hand
that kept you all the while
believing as you wished.
A world that long was yours
before it was revealed –
imagination soars
with courage its master.
Flowers filling a place
left bereft of your own,
a portrait in a vase
found by me, your daughter.

Stolen Fruit

Will the fruit be wasted?
Fully ripened, hanging heavy,
unpicked
not unchosen.

Blackbird, blackbird
bowing to temptation,
tasting before
the deer,
sudden snows,
or inevitable decomposition
steal it from sight.

Alyson Faye

Alyson originally trained as a teacher/tutor. While living and working in Birmingham in the UK she wrote poetry, a children's book, *Soldiers in the Mist* published by Collins, and a short story published by Ginn and Company.

She now lives near Brontë country in Yorkshire with her teen son, partner and three rescue cats. She writes noir flash fiction which appears online at horrortree.com, zeroflash and Tubeflash; in anthologies published by Raging Aardvark and Three Drops from a Cauldron; and as podcasts. Her story for teens, *The Nearly Boy*, is available online from Alfie Dog Fiction. Alyson enjoys old movies, singing, and swimming. She is a confirmed chocoholic and still hopeless at maths.

Her blog can be accessed on request at:
www.alysonfayewordpress.wordpress.com

Very Like Vermeer

'You remind me of a Vermeer lady,'
he whispered in my ear, one lazy day.
'Where she stands by the window, solemn faced.'
He took my image, posting on his blog.
Model. Mistress. Muse; love sealed with a click.
Courts me in his cavalier fashion,
texting, tweeting, here, there, always dashing –
his life a game of chess; mine solitaire.
I, a brown mouse, without him, sit, read, write.
Researching his beloved Vermeer girls.
A shadowy man, whose legacy was
kids, debts, dreams; of home, hearth and harpsichords,
drawn out on checker boards, in black and white.
I grow, full-bellied. Expectant. Waiting.

Rooks' Flight

Daylight dribbles into dusk,
We fly together
rimming the hard edges,
skimming the soft bloom
of shadows.

We rest, roost on chimneys,
spires, feast on icy landscapes.
We are never alone.
We flock in rowdy gaggles.

Our paths are a
crazy map of near misses.
We are programmed pilots
of our own journey.
We fly to live.

Others drift away. We stay, endure
winter's hard breathy edge.
We cling to what is left;
the grounds' crackling rind.

Darkness creeps,
caressing our wings,
clenching at our hearts.
On one beat, we turn,
rallying us. Memory tugs us

to the branches' tracery,
wherein we rest.

The Poppy Parade

Stone cold, battle deafened,
we lie, hunkered down,
waist deep in mud,
our tiny tight knit battalion.
Resting but restless,
waiting for the order
dreading the dawn.

Some prayed,
or wrote letters home,
'My dearest, darling....'
Some stared blank eyed,
whilst others wept
at sights never to be unseen.

This flat field of mud
where only the sky
and its stars witness
the slaughter of youth
with all its joy and hope.

A few, too few returning,
recount tales which hardly
bear hearing.
The courage of the fallen
remembered in the poppy parade.

Bruce Goodman

Bruce Goodman is a New Zealander, now retired from working in schools.

He describes himself as 'unpublished', but his over 60 plays for children, teenagers, and adults have seen several thousand productions on stage courtesy of the photocopier.

His writings are available at http://stagebarn.com/ and include a biography, *Bits of a Boyhood*, about growing up in rural New Zealand, and a novel titled *A Passing Shower*. His blog of 1001 stories and counting, plus 101 music compositions, are freely available at https://weaveaweb.wordpress.com/

Bury Me Flamboyantly Clad

Bury me flamboyantly clad.
No white silk shroud for me,
no brown and heavy sacking.
The Hawaiian shirt in the bottom drawer might do the trick
although I wouldn't be seen dead in it while living.

Bury me flamboyantly clad.
The purple underwear perhaps,
with bright pink elastic bands.
You know the one? The faded writing used to read,
"Down dog! Down!" It's quite unused for years.

Bury me flamboyantly clad.
No naked skin below the naval,
no hatless head with balding patch.
Green golfing trousers and yellow baseball cap.
Unironed one hopes; a bit of plaid; reverse the cap.

Bury me flamboyantly clad.
No history digger in a thousand years
must dig me up for study and say,
"Put this body back in earth." No! No! He needs must say:
"Holy mackerel! Oh my God! Fetch the glass cabinet!"

It's Pretty

A Pantoum

It's pretty but there's no hope
in the picture on a jigsaw box;
patched, thatched, and always a puzzle,
and a couple of ducks on a lake.

In the picture on a jigsaw box
there's always lots and lots of flowers,
and a couple of ducks on a lake
with lots and lots of babies.

There's always lots and lots of flowers
and those inside the house
with lots and lots of babies,
can't feed them all.

And those inside the house,
they've gone to pieces,
can't feed them all
in bits and pieces.

They've gone to pieces,
jigsawed into shape
in bits and pieces,
disintegrated and broken.

Jigsawed into shape,
patched, thatched, and always a puzzle,
disintegrated and broken.
It's pretty, but there's no hope.

Helen Harrison

Helen was raised on the Wirral, seven miles from Liverpool in the UK, by Irish parents, and has lived most of her adult life in Co Monaghan, Ireland. She is married with a grown-up daughter and enjoys travelling, and reading poetry at various venues.

Her poems have been published in *Live Encounters Poetry*, *The Poetry Shed*, *A New Ulster*, *Poethead*, *North West Words*, *Mad Swirl*, *Algebra of Owls*, *Tintean*, *The Galway Review*, *Bray Journal* and *Stanzas*.

Her first collection of poetry, *The Last Fire*, was published in 2015 by Lapwing. (https://sites.google.com/a/lapwingpublications.com/lapwing-store/helen-harrison)

Some of Helen's poems can be found at http://poetry4on.blogspot.ie/

Mum and Spuds

How are you managing for heating oil?
Do you know that Mrs Mullen died?
I hope you like onions with your stuffing?
You said in your text that you're on nights next.

Heaped on offerings of food,
Hot pans make mood for flavour.
Television. Loud repeated soaps,
Water hissing on stove. Potato
Peelings blocking sink – no time to think;

Can I help? I question her red face,
No, it's alright – clean the windows instead –
but listen; wait until after you're fed.

The Rhythm of Wood

'Hazel burns well – made for fire.
Ash splits and cuts easily. The thorn
Is the best. Elders are useless,' he gestures
Through gaps. His hands are veined
Like leaves, he touches his cap in thought.

He is a character from this town land;
Born of the substance of soil,
His pride in wood-piles.

A shy bachelor smile – and dragging a branch,
Comments on the cold March – his furrowed brow
Like his fields are full with life, and worn with the
Tread of time, fertilized with the rapture of repetition,
Feeds his ragged trouser philanthropy?

Forty acres with a rose-scented doorway to the past,
At last, reconciled to being a bachelor and a good
Neighbour. I smile gratitude for his earthy routine –
The rhythm of wood freely given.

Judith Highcock

Born in Lancashire in the UK, Judith now lives in Otley, West Yorkshire. She has been writing poetry for over 30 years, mainly for her own pleasure and for the entertainment of friends. However, as Judith explains: 'Recently I have been trying to take it a bit more seriously – possibly something to do with getting older!'

So far, her work has appeared in two anthologies and her ambition is to have a collection published.

When not writing poetry, she spends her time playing Crown Green Bowls and is a proud member of the West Yorkshire County short mat bowls team.

Mount Pisgah

Aldebaran rises over Mount Pisgah
Orion chasing
in winter blue sky
darker than expected
darkness also heart deep
stillness too

In the still of the dark blue night
something is hunting

And like Eve I fall
absorbed into the hum
the drum beat; the song
and then the silence

Mid-Winter Landscape

the silence of snow

only the owl bears witness
to this covering of solitude

the sun makes no
impression on the
monochrome scene

the hill crouches in shadow
its trees shocked and frozen in place
no breeze stirs leafless
branches

not even the north wind
dares to disturb this mid-
winter's dream

how cold will it be when night falls?

The Beach

Deserted beach
sunset
warm breeze
caressing

sand beneath bare feet
waves lapping against stones
seaweed, shoes and souls
adrift in the foam

sadness and salt
wet on my face
as the sun sinks
into the sea

the tide turns
as I turn away

Cynthia Jobin

The American poet Cynthia Jobin died in late 2016. It was Cynthia who suggested the title of this anthology and her poems are indeed jewels, waiting to be discovered. By the time of her death, her poetry had attracted many admirers; it richly deserves even wider attention. The poems included here were selected by Cynthia for this anthology before she died.

Immediately after graduating, Cynthia taught in private and public schools. As she explains on her poetry blog: 'After seven years, I left that work because I wanted to "be a writer" (*Cynthia's quotation marks*) ... In those years I did many odd jobs, worked in community theatre and learned the traditional craft of calligraphy ... My ultimate job, from which I finally retired, was as an adjunct professor of graduate students, lecturing in history, aesthetics and research at the Massachusetts College of Art and Design. I still consider my vocation that of poet. And now, that's what I do: I read and write poems.'

Cynthia was also a warm and generous supporter of other writers. A wide selection of her work can be found at https://littleoldladywho.net/

The Sun Also Sets

Without a bedtime story or a lullaby
the evening's blush sinks to a deeper red
then slips into a slit between the earth and sky
leaving our goodbyes lingering, unsaid.

I do not want to go, or let you go.
I want to dare this ending, call its bluff,
delay our parting with a sudden overflow
of words – too many and yet not enough –

while you, my dearest one, would choose
blunt disappearance, the mute way
to stanch an agony – those deeper blues
along the skyline fire – as if to say

the sun rises, the sun also sets.
So let it set. Let us let it. Let's.

Ode to a Condiment

From the trusty crock you teach
how cold a winter's morning
or how warm a summer's day might be.
Oh not in thermometric numbers by degree
but by your suave substantial answer
to the knife tip's touch,
by your complexion and your spreadability.

At your most noble, taken new
from finest milk and churned
to a consistency all of your own,
epitome of softness and a cache
of flavor---you're unsalted, sweet,
delicately of the pasture: dandelion,
clover or alfalfa, onion grass...

I love yourself
by any means conveyed –
a raft of toast, a lobster tail,
an artichoke sautéed – even my cat
demands a tiny pat of you each day.
But best of all, pièce de resistance,
those days when I bake bread

I break a hunk
warm, before the loaf is sliced,
and slather you all over it.
Then you are paradise.

Getting It

For many years you don't get it.
You know you haven't gotten it.
But there's still time and
maybe you'll get it.

You cultivate the persons, places,
things that appear to have it.
What you get there is proof
that you still don't get it.

It's above you, beyond you.
It's all Greek, which you don't speak.
You need more experience,
you need more education.

You need the magic formula,
the password, the key.
You need a teacher, a mentor,
a confidante, confessor, referee.

You have tried hard,
been nice to people –
maybe nicer than you should.
How long can this go on?

Until you don't care anymore.
Then in a desert breeze,

a written word, a flower's heart,
you hear the temple gong:

you already have it,
you've had it all along.

Marianne Jones

Marianne is a retired teacher, actor, and choir director from the wilds of Northwestern Ontario in Canada. She and her husband Reg have two amazing daughters and two gorgeous granddaughters.

Although not all her words are carved in stone, three of her poems are: in permanent installation at Prince Arthur's Landing at Marina Park in Thunder Bay.

Her poetry has won awards from Writers' Digest, The Word Guild, Utmost Christian Writers, and Northwestern Ontario Writers Workshop. It has appeared in numerous literary and denominational publications and anthologies.

Marianne's books include: *The Girl Who Wouldn't Die*, *The Serenity Stone Murder*, and *Great Grandma's Gifts*, all available on Amazon.

Her website is http://www.mariannejones.net

Spring Cleaning

Clean my house, Lord.
Come into my closets and start pitching:
that old, out-of-date fear,
that family heirloom resentment
passed through generations,
that worry
that seemed like such a good purchase,
that trunk I don't even want to open – pitch it, Lord.
Sweep away cobwebs
of pride and ambition.
Leave nothing untouched.
Throw open the windows.
Let the Spirit-Breeze sweeten the stale air.
Pour your sunlight
into the dark corners where depression broods.
Don't let me take anything back, saying,
"I might need this someday."

The Romantic

God is a romantic. He believes in lost causes,
hopeless cases,
impossible dreams.
Unlike the hard-headed pragmatist,
He forgives the unforgivable,
loves the unlovable,
and heals those broken past mending.

Vanessa Kirkpatrick

Vanessa Kirkpatrick's first collection, *To Catch the Light*, won the inaugural John Knight Memorial Poetry Manuscript Prize and was Commended for the Anne Elder Award (2013).

Her second collection, *The Conversation of Trees*, was published by Hope Street Press (2017), and her poetry has been featured on national radio.

Vanessa has a PhD in English Literature from the University of Sydney and is an experienced workshop facilitator and creative writing mentor.

She lives in the Blue Mountains, Australia.

Apple

for Sasha

Now you can point and say the word.

You chant round vowels, crisp
consonants, feel the fullness of 'apple'
purling on your tongue.

It's taken from the fruit bowl,
sweet word made sweeter apple flesh,
and placed into your small, eager hands.

You clasp the shining prize
and set to the task of eating
with concentrated purpose.

What do you hold but arms of sun
pouring sheaves of wheaten gold
through clouds and leaves

until skin blushed from touching?
What do you savour on your tongue
but clandestine imprints from the feet of bees,

and the waxing, waning moon
feeding earthly spheres
with memories of ancient paradise?

You roll in the grass of your dreams
and say it over in your sleep,
tasting the sweetness of syllables,

those red orbs tumbling through the sky.

Wittstock, 1946

in memory of my great-grandmother, Helmi Reinhardt

Helmi walks to the railway tracks.
She carries the memory of her three children
and husband. Like a bunch of fragile roses
clasped to her chest. She doesn't feel
the cold, though the air she breathes
is like ice in her lungs.

Snow falls on the lost lagoons of Ingria,
the frozen hillsides of her childhood home.
She recalls the parsonage
flanked by birches, elm and spruce.
Feels her feet running
in brown lace-up boots
as she chases her sisters –
Alma, Edit, Fanni and Hilma –
braids flying, shadows long
in the last of the midwinter sun.

Here in Wittstock, she feels
she has seen the last of the sun.
She glances upwards, sees
the crane's abandoned nest,

a clutch of sticks balanced
on an unused chimney.

Her coat snags as she climbs
the low fence to the tracks.
She surveys the straight lines
with their cold iron purpose.
Thinks of Rudolf, her youngest son,
how his violin lies mute
within its smooth wooden case.
She has covered it in a blanket,
as if to keep it warm.

She kneels at the tracks,
thinks of whispering a prayer
to the mute and cloudless sky.
But here – in her place –
is a small loaf of bread.
It steams, like her breath
that opens and closes. A gift
from nowhere, a small reprieve.

And so her days once again
promise to open and close,
for better, for worse.

Helmi climbs back over the fence.
She hurries past rows of closed doors,
small squares of anonymous lights,
past the still bells of the *Marien Kirche*.

The warm loaf she folds in her arms,
as if shielding a child
from the oncoming night.

Leaving

in memory of my grandmother

Beneath the weeping birch,
I crouch at the foothills of listening.
The leaves whisper themselves undone
as they tread the air
for the first last time.

Afternoon light sifts memories:
my daughter, not knowing
the words for leaving this life,
brought you blankets and pillows.

Steeped in the warm vernacular of touch,
she climbed onto your bed,
placed her hand in the wisps of your hair,
pressed her mouth with tenderness
to the dip in your cheek.
Gute Nacht, Good night.

Betula pendula 'Tristis'.
My mother planted this birch
outside your bedroom window.
In spring, each leaf unfolds

its promises, letters of hope,
in verdant green.
Winter, she is *mater dolorosa*,
long arms bent in sorrow,
emptied of prayer.

The wind keens through the branches.
The leaves whisper themselves undone
as they tread the air
for the first last time.

Previously published in *Communion Journal*, Dec 2016.

Jim Kleinhenz

Jim lives in New York City, right across the street from the United Nations in an area known as Tudor City.

He taught at City College for a number of years; before that he was a building super, a handyman, a finish carpenter, and a maker of fine wooden boxes.

He started writing poetry in 2008 and has been writing steadily ever since. His poems can be found at www.extrasimile.wordpress.com

He was diagnosed with Parkinson's disease 11 years ago.

Milk by Morning

It's nighttime on the farm.
What has this to do with bees buzzing?
With meadows moaning?
With truth bubbling up in sentences
from ponds delighted to be here at all?
Even the silence grows dense.
The cows nod sagely as they dream.
All this will be milk by morning.

Pavane Pour une Infante Défunte

Each year I hold her ancient body in my arms
as if she were a little child again. I tell
her not to listen to the sound the river makes
behind the clouds and fog. We'll pretend it's
only the sun the hills have hidden, not the words
we can no longer read. We'll pretend sunshine is
neither a song nor a poem. You must listen only
to my voice, I tell her; not to its whisper.

And so each year we add to her mysterious poem.
Each year she trembles in my arm,
once again my captive. Her muscles fade
into what they must stand for –

Your dreams defy death as night ends,
I whisper. *You aren't really asleep.*

Pavane pour une infante défunte (*Pavane for a dead infanta*) is a piece of music for solo piano written by the French composer Maurice Ravel in 1899. In Ravel's words, it is an 'evocation of a pavane that a little princess might, in former times, have danced at the Spanish court'. The pavane was a slow processional dance very popular in the courts of Europe in the sixteenth and seventeenth centuries.

Elizabeth Leaper

Elizabeth is a writer, poet and illustrator who has enjoyed writing since she was a small child. Her work has been broadcast on BBC radio and she has had stories, poems and articles published in several anthologies and small press magazines.

A former primary school teacher, Elizabeth writes prose and poetry for both children and adults, and runs a small independent publishing company, Silverburn Publishing, based in Staffordshire in the UK. Profits from the sale of her books are donated to charity.

Visit Silverburn Publishing:
http://silverburnpublishing.co.uk

About Morning

This was going to be a poem about morning
but since I am writing it in the early afternoon
with the sun slanting through the slatted fence
and between the trees, casting striations of brightness
across the lawn and memories of warm
sunny days, it is hard to remember the dawn.

A shaft of sunlight through the window
and across the page, where my pen crawls ant-like
in its ramblings, draws my attention. I look up
and from the corner of my eye catch a glimpse
of flashing flame on the trunk of a newly-bare
but unknown tree in my neighbour's garden.

This warrants closer inspection and I turn
with full attention to the realisation that what I see
is nothing but the prism effect of the sun filtering
through the branches of the firs, focusing the darker,
more vibrant ranges of the spectrum in reds, purples,
oranges and yellows, in semblance of flames on the trunk.

I scroll my eyes down to the lawn in the shaded northern
corner of the garden, where the frost still lies white
on the grass and instantly I am transported back to morning –
Gauzy grey clouds cover much of the sky but to the northeast
chill pale blue like an over-diluted watercolour wash
stains the sky, speckled with clouds in icy-pink like candyfloss.

A winter sky in late autumn, frost covers all and dawn stands shivering on the doorstep. The birds find it too much effort to sing and the comforting cooing of the doves is absent. Now I put down my pen and step outside into the warmth of the sunshine. It is a lie. It is much colder than I thought and I prefer the honest truth of the icy-cold morning.

Old Photographs

There is something about old photographs
that draws the eye;
not just the faded edges, sepia tones,
fuzzy images, but something more.
We cannot pass them by without a look.
Are we yearning for those days long gone
or do we hope to see a place we recognise,
maybe a face, and if we do to then say
'My, how things have changed,
it isn't like that now'? and we laugh
at the old-fashioned mode of dress.

Something about old photographs
brings a sigh.
Family photographs are the best
and worst of all. We wonder
where and when it was, who
took the picture that records the scene.
Who is that boy with Great Aunt Jean?
Could it be her son, killed in the war?
And that young girl looking shy
beside the cottage door, do you think
it could be Aunty Clare?

We study the faces,
search these glimpses of the past,
wish that we could give them names,

we question; all the time aware
that there can be no answers now —
there is no one left to ask.

Lambing

Here in the middle of a winter's night,
darkly-light with frost and bitter cold,
while bold Orion stalks across the sky
watching where the stellar bear
points towards the far North Star,
we sit on a straw bale side by side
in that dreamlike state, both wide awake
and yet still half-asleep. Our languid gaze
takes in the pens of ewes and lambs
snuggled in cosiness, twitching in sleep.

The newest born have just arrived,
I hock-carried them up from Woody Hollow,
slippery, slickly wet, while you enticed
the dam to follow across the frost-rimed field.
Now she licks them, mothering, nickering
in response to their high-pitched bleats.
The lambs struggling to their feet, stand
all wobbly-legs and wire-wool coats,
take their first taste of nourishment,
then settle down contentedly to sleep.

Warm steam rises from the fleeces,
warm breath mists the cold night air.
We've washed our ice-cold fingers
under the tap and in the living sheep-skin
warmed and dried them buried deep.

Sitting here we do not feel the cold,
among the summer-fragrance of the hay,
the steady sound of munching, little bleats
of sleepfullness and in this time for dreams
there is only you, and me, and sheep.

This poem won first prize in the Salopean Poetry Society's Members Only Poetry Competition in 2013.

John Looker

John lives with his wife in Surrey, south-east England, and has been writing poetry all his life. Now retired, he worked for 40 years in the British civil service. He has travelled extensively, both professionally and privately, and his wide and varied experience provides a rich resource for his poetry.

The Human Hive, John's first collection of poetry, was published in 2015 by Bennison Books and was selected by the Poetry Library for the UK's national collection. His poems have appeared in print and in online journals, have been read on local radio and were included in *When Time and Space Conspire,* an anthology commemorating the 25th anniversary of the Austin International Poetry Festival. He is also a regular contributor to *The Wagon*, a literary journal published monthly in India.

The *Poetry from John Looker* website is at https://johnstevensjs.wordpress.com ('John Looker' being a pseudonym in tribute to a grandfather).

Newborn

to Beth

Until this moment, little apprentice person,
dwelling as you were within the womb,
      it would have been touch,
your fingers fluttering, your limbs
probing all the frontiers of your realm.

And hearing too, your mother's heart and lungs
thundering like a mill or an engine house.
      Then something else,
something that you learnt slowly
and lovingly, like a musical score: her voice.

Just look at you now, our little explorer,
finding out about eyes, discovering light;
      and colour; and movement;
and your mother's adoring smile.
Just look at you here, at dawn on the shore of your life.

The Perfectionist

My father did that, he said;
my father was the one to ensure
that all the lines were true.
And she raised her eyes to the tiled expanse
of the end elevation of the mall.

She could picture him up there, high
on scaffolding where arctic winds
came riding in with their spurs.
Spirit level. Plumb line. The radio off,
except when he stopped for lunch.

And she thought of the Taj Mahal,
the golden Dome of the Rock,
and men in Byzantium long ago
cutting their tiny mozaics
for the ceiling of Hagia Sophia.

This is a new poem on the theme of looking at life through work, which is the subject of John's first poetry collection, The Human Hive, *published by Bennison Books.*

The Escape to Troy

Rising to her feet, Helen of the plump white arms
was well aware of the eyes,
from the helmsman behind her to the officers at their stations
and all the men at their oars.

She was silhouetted against the evening sun:
that head to eclipse men's wives,
those hips that could found a dynasty
rocking to the rhythm of the waves.

She had turned her back on Sparta,
the provincial court which once seemed full of promise,
the undistinguished dwellings, the husband
with his hearty companions and predictable habits.

Beneath her the keel of the ship leapt. She swayed
bountifully under the gaze of those eyes,
turning towards her prince, her chosen abductor,
placing a manicured hand on his hairless arm.

Behind her, she knew, all was confusion, dismay.
But the ship sprang forward, light as a bird in the breeze,
firm as the back of a whale in the flying spray,
sailing wherever she – or the gods – might please.

The land ahead lay pink with almond groves
and green with rows of the vine. There were boys

tending goats. And there on a hill – now gold
in the setting sun – were the walls and the towers of Troy.

This is a new poem from John's next collection of poetry, Shimmering Horizons,
to be published by Bennison Books.

And to a Winter's Day Also ...

(for Frances)

... for isn't there beauty in a winter's day?
Not just the frail sunlight sparkling on ice,
the clear skies, the dark holly with those dear
berries; nor even the breathtaking lace
of trees in the cold air. Give these their due
but there is more – for all is stillness; peace.
  Walking, you take my arm, and I am yours.

A.J. Mark

Anna is an elementary school teacher. She lives north of Guelph, Ontario, with her husband and two daughters. She also teaches yoga movement classes through her business, Spacious Place Yoga.

Along with other beloved pleasures, like long walks and travel, Anna writes poetry and has a blog which can be accessed on request:
fromaflower.wordpress.com

Angel in the Snow

She is our transference of heaven,
A stunning imitation of light,

With the moon and stars she fills,
Gazes longingly at the sky and sings,

Freedom! Implores, *Ignite! Ignite!* and
Smothers the sparks with her wings.

Why such a mundane, carnal end
For one who dares touch the intangible,

Express the inexpressible? Serene,
Her angelic form, bound to earth by our

Concave impressions, disappears in the
Same mysterious way that a deer's

Carcass isn't seen decomposing, yet
Walking through the wood we know

Green is the vibrancy of her decay,
White the sheen of an angel's reflection.

The Timbre of Frost

I placed the kettle on the stove and heard
the steam's rising speed and pitch;

I felt the agitation of music inside a chamber
and enjoyed knowing, through sounds,

the moment to lift the stainless vessel
off the red spiral – just before the scream.

Later, I saw frost bloom across the window,
a spontaneous crystalline fire,

the fractals' perfect chaotic symmetry,
a burst of delicate flame-like ferns

– and traced their piercing cry.

Lanterns

Let us read poetry by a window
and have no lights on inside but angle the book,
tilt the page to face the light, the light of our fading day,
the day we can still feel working in our limbs, and smell
on our skin and hair; the window is our memory of it.
Let us have this day spread across some timeless words,
words we read until the moment they merge into our darkened
surroundings, strange shapes born of this confluence,
and carry all of it into our night.

Frédéric G. Martin

Frédéric was born in 1968, in Paris, France. He is a teacher and teaches French, his mother tongue.

A language lover, he writes poems in both English and French. He blogs at https://wordsinthelight.com/

Between Chatou and Croissy

I was walking along the Seine
between Chatou and Croissy
admiring upright hollyhocks
as proud as poor,

sunlight dancing on water,
trees by the riverside,
and pretty houses
with closed shutters,

when suddenly
and so mysteriously
I ran into Renoir's ghost
and saw the Light again.

Forgotten Sandcastles

Starfishes
or silver shells,
sea glass pebbles,
blue-green diamonds.

A lost dolphin's dream,
an angel walking on water,
or maybe the key that opens
all forgotten sandcastles.

Will we ever know
what a child
running on the beach
is looking for?

Chris McLoughlin

Chris is a performance poet, writer and workshop facilitator based in Nottingham in the UK. He has performed at many venues, including at Staatstheater, Braunschweig (Germany), Greenwich & Docklands Festival, Nottingham Poetry Festival, and Luton International Carnival.

Chris' writing focuses primarily on mental health and enabling others to discuss grief through writing. His aim is to create a platform for those suffering silently, and for readers and audiences to feel less alone.

He has a Distinction in MA Creative Writing from the University of Nottingham, was Artistic Director of *Mouthy Poets*, and is now pursuing a full-time career in writing. He performs internationally, and enables young people's voices through poetry around the UK. He is currently preparing his first full collection, *Underneath the Almond Tree*.

For more on Chris, or to purchase his first chapbook **Break***down*, visit www.Pijaykin.com

Pijaykin

for the Mouthy ones

On the first day of secondary school, I drew my Pijaykin.

A Pijaykin is a small flame, with big eyes, short legs,
odd hands (I never could draw hands). There's a Pijaykin
inside each of us. They can be different shapes, sizes,
colours. Mine was blue, buried beneath my ribcage.

My teacher told me my Pijaykin was wrong,
that we were being tested on **real** mythical creatures.
I wanted to ask *What's a **real** mythical creature?*
but instead I said
He is real
to me.

When I got caught throwing mud through the library window
my Pijaykin told me *it's okay to make mistakes.*
When Sean Seavey put gum in my hair,
my Pijaykin didn't laugh.
When I failed Physics A-level,
my Pijaykin told me *gravity is only a theory, anyway.*

But a flame needs fuel.

After eighteen years of multiple choices,
never getting any *real* choices,
scolded for making my own answers,

I was sure my flame was gone,
doused by *Don't, Can't,*
Not Like That

I was wrong.
It was still there, buried beneath my ribcage
with big eyes, short legs, odd hands
(I still can't draw hands).

And it found them.

Other flames drawn together,
red, purple, gold, green,
lost, low, nearly out,
but when one would flicker
threatening to fall cold,
another would share its warmth.

That's the thing with Pijaykins.
They don't die. It only takes
one touch from another's flame,

and yours is given life again.

Chris Moran

Chris lives in Leeds in the UK. She recovered from alcoholism and the depths of despair, only to be faced with a long-delayed diagnosis of multiple sclerosis. The diagnosis freed her spirit and unlocked her creativity.

Her poetry documents her life with courageous honesty, unexpected humour, and a clear and unwavering eye. She has now enjoyed many years of contented sobriety after attending an Alcoholics Anonymous programme. Her poetry touches many people worldwide who feel she speaks directly to them and their own experiences of life.

In her own words: 'Life is too short for it to be filled with anger; it can always be beautiful if we allow it to be. Every moment counts, good and bad, and I want to live them all to the full, not just wade my way through. This is now my time, not only to survive, but to thrive.'

Chris's first collection *Dancing in the Rain* is published by Bennison Books. Her poetry can also be found at https://journeyintopoetry.wordpress.com/

Dad's Hat

It sits on the kitchen table like
a huge bird, motionless,
protecting its young,
a light brooding patch
where it has worn thin.

It's been there for three weeks now.

I pluck a small feather of courage
from the anguished air,
ask if I could perhaps put it away.
Her sharp-edged words pierce
my sleeping loss and it stirs.

I make more tea;
she sits squarely on his chair,
knits a few more ounces of grief
into the last few stitches
of a sleeve,
as a vagrant star peers
through the window
at the close of another
wounded day.

Past Lives

He takes his little brother's hand;
they sit by the window,
contemplate family photos on the sill.
There is no one else here;
the room seems like a deep secret
they both promise to keep.
That's you when you were a baby,
says the older one,
that's what you looked like.
Yes, says the younger, that's me.
It's almost as if they have been here before.
They stare at the sudden summer rain
pelting against the glass,
both silent,
recalling past lives.

Crying Over Spilt Tea

This morning I spilt a full cup of tea
over the bed;
my hand simply gave way.
It happens.
Everything soaked through
including myself, and

you, the stoical carer
already overloaded with
extra chores, and a time schedule
that used to belong to me,
rose calmly to the challenge,
stripped the bed,
placed stained linen carefully to soak
and went out the door
to collect our grandson
for the day.

From the corner of my eye
I could see it – disability
sitting on the sidelines
gloating, large as life
with a smugness I could have slapped.

Sometimes I feel like a child.

But unlike a child,

I watched your face as you
cleared the mess;
the pursed lips, unassailable truth
in the extra crease on a forehead,
that said
this wasn't on today's list.

We said nothing;
silence grew louder
until we both heard it –
the sadness, sobbing softly
for our loss.

Anna Mosca

Anna Mosca is the author of three poetry books and her work has been featured in numerous anthologies.

Her poetry blog, www.anna mosca.com, is widely followed from all over the world. A former professor of art and photography, Anna spends winter in Indian Wells in California, enjoying the desert and its awesome light, and summer in Northern Italy, where she grows her own vegetable garden and attends her many poetry engagements.

Anna's current published work is *California Notebooks* Volume 01 and Volume 02. These two bilingual compilations of poems, in English and Italian, were published in 2015 and 2016 and can be easily found online or in local libraries.

Stories Within Lines

lost count of all
the unconscious
glances reaped
today in the crowd

with those open
half smiles the west
comes with so many
stories within lines

scars or tattoos
step after step
walking the city
subway line again

No Hands

as everything crashes
on us tall dreams columns
and all the bridges you

quietly burned retina
fails me it seems I can't
see clearly anything

or find the reasons
there's some space now
between my vision

and what needs to be
in focus I blur away
as piercing memories

will do as well as
they'll wash down the

drain inch by inch

the hair I grew while
loving you coarse
now by lack of tender

touches to some pet
you wanted to keep close
to yourself maybe not

you had no hands lately

I still can't find
a reason to war concern
eating on me

Beautiful Beauty

moving from silence
to silence landing
from airport to airport
friends a crown
on my head to be
proud of life as
beautiful beauty
surely can be

Robert Okaji

The son of a career soldier, Robert moved from place to place throughout his childhood. He holds a BA in History from The University of Texas at Austin, served without distinction in the U.S. Navy, lived the hand-to-mouth existence of a bookstore owner, and worked in a library and as a university administrator.

He lives in Texas with his wife, two dogs, some books and a beverage refrigerator stocked with craft beer.

Recent publications include the chapbook, *If Your Matter Could Reform* (Dink Press), two micro-chapbooks, *You Break What Falls* and *No Eye but the Moon's: Adaptations from the Chinese* (Origami Poems Project), a mini-digital chapbook, *Interval's Night* (Platypus Press), and 'The Circumference of Other', a collection appearing in *Ides: A Collection of Poetry Chapbooks* (Silver Birch Press).

His work has appeared in *Taos Journal of International Poetry & Art*, *Boston Review*, *Hermeneutic Chaos*, *Glass: A Journal of Poetry*, *Panoply*, *Eclectica*, *Clade Song*, *Into the Void*, *High Window*, *West Texas Literary Review* and elsewhere. Visit his blog, *O at the Edges*, at http://robertokaji.com/

How to Write a Poem

Learn to curse in three languages. When midday
yawns stack high and your eyelids flutter, fire up

the chain saw; there's always something to dismember.
Make it new. Fear no bridges. Accelerate through

curves, and look twice before leaping over fires,
much less into them. Read bones, read leaves, read

the dust on shelves and commit to memory a thousand
discarded lines. Next, torch them. Take more than you

need, buy books, scratch notes in the dirt and watch
them scatter down nameless alleys at the evening's first

gusts. Gather words and courtesies. Guard them carefully.
Play with others, observe birds, insects and neighbours,

but covet your minutes alone and handle with bare hands
only those snakes you know. Mourn the kindling you create

and toast each new moon as if it might be the last one
to tug your personal tides. When driving, sing with the radio.

Always. Turn around instead of right. Deny ambition.
Remember the freckles on your first love's left breast.

There are no one-way streets. Appreciate the fragrance
of fresh dog crap while scraping it from the boot's sole.

Steal, don't borrow. Murder your darlings and don't get
caught. Know nothing, but know it well. Speak softly

and thank the grocery store clerk for wishing you
a nice day even if she didn't mean it. Then mow the grass,

grill vegetables, eat, laugh, wash dishes, talk, bathe,
kiss loved ones, sleep, dream, wake. Do it all again.

Hail

My hands know the sadness of rock,
of unfinished lines and rough

sides tapering to sharpness.
The shape of solitude, turning.

Now the stones fall as water,
a woman lets down her hair

and laughter chokes through silence.
Into this dream I descend.

Arthritis

If at night I stray in thought,
dreaming of nimble fingers

and my departed dog's walk,
will you smile

when I scratch his absent ear
and apologise for the times

I failed him? Even combined,
all the words in these unread books

could never match the joy of jumping
for the kicked ball, no matter the

outcome, despite the consequences.

Jim Winton Porter

Jim lives near the ocean in NSW, Australia. He is an actor as well as a writer.

The ocean has been a part of his life forever, even before he was born. He comes from Polynesian ancestry and his father was a sailor. The great loves of his life are: his family – three sons, Khan, Dante and Cosmo; his partner and muse, Hanni; and creativity – which includes sporadic bursts of writing, surfing, exercise (he describes this as solving the puzzle of human maximum effortless energy production) and exploring the mysterious intricacies of this life.

More of his prose and poetry can be found at thearthriticsurfer.com

Biology

We begin as 300,000,000 swimmers.

What invisible currents wrap their fingers and pull our bodies north?

Cocooned by the original Red Sea.

A scent, a taste, biology says.

'Radiance of Desire'? 'Hint of Secret Skin'?

'Lily of the Valley!' a daughter remembers.

Breath for divers: a scent to die for.

Frangipani and sea salt on a tongue, she knows, compels many to undulate upwards, not towards the sky, or the light, but up inside of her, where it is dark, through the fragile layers, against the sweeping blood cilia tide, until they dance – the last swimmer and the hidden perfect lotus.

'Essence of Love,' I believe.

Winged Crosses

Wooden crosses lipped by flowers.
At the edges of the road in the grass, with the dead trees and
    the broken fence lines.
The ache of names glimpsed in passing. Strangers: fathers,
    mothers, daughters and sons.
Creating sacred spaces along the highway heading west into
    the sun.
The desolate bodies beside the road. Real. And imagined.
Above us on this road the hovering winged crosses. Or are
    they angels?
Descending through the crystal shimmering air to lift the
    flesh
for one last flight: The consolation of death by accident.

Two Nights

One

As I sit up in bed
The clock's red eyes read 2.30,
There's the breath of fear at my spine
And there are glittering stars
Outside the window above my head
And there's the howl of a car.
And I'm thinking of you on a mattress …
On the floor in her lounge room …
Where patience has become a penance,
Staring at the white ceiling
Listening to her breathing …
Waiting for footsteps or words …
Then fear casts its light
And I realise that courage is really
Another word for kindness.

Two

Lying in the dark
Unable to sleep
My body's boundaries
Invaded by pain
Watching the light
Across the ceiling
Sliding like water.
Caressing me.

Holding on to a memory of before the
Invasion
When sleep was a refuge and I knew that
My body was a landscape of possibilities and unfulfilled
Fantasies.
Where did you go? I whisper.
I went away to show you, instruct you in the gift of this. The
preciousness of this ...
Your life. You pass through here only once.
And it's as if I'm
Peering at a stranger's body
Inspecting it, picking it to pieces, the molecules and cells
The life lines disappearing into
The wilderness and expanse of flesh.
The uncertainty and fragility.
And the wonder of destruction and resurrection.
Where have you been? She asked.
Nowhere and everywhere.
Well ... welcome back ... welcome home.

Jean Rodenbough

Jean is a retired Presbyterian pastor, a poet, and also a prose writer. She lives in Greensboro in the United States and has four children and eight grandchildren.

All Things That Matter Press has published two of her books, *Rachel's Children: Surviving the Second World War* and *Bebe & Friends: Tails of Rescue*. She has also self-published several books.

She blogs at http://jeansblender.blogspot.co.uk/

Water

reflects stars formed in galaxies with light
from creation to dance upon its surfaces
so that planets begin and I swim into life

water fills mouths in deserts and high places
claims its existence, deadly in its absence
or when filled with poisons but alive even so

in lakes, oceans, brooks, rainfalls, the place
where I drench my body, swim in waters
I can touch but not hold, cherish by faith

today I savour its star-gifted clarity from a glass,
my human quest in this survival story of life;
may its gift quench thirst for more than water

I lift my eyes to the light of a sun centred
upon a sea of orbiting liquid necessity
in the universe where a gift of water

still offers the wet ancient mystery
and possibility of renewing life
we are assuaged, drink our fill

After Snow

I remember child years in snow
those deep white chilled layers
memory of slow falling flakes
to ground frozen in beauty

I go out to feel silent cold
see reflected whiteness
smell the sweet clean air
it holds me in its stillness
and the silence
the silence

As Nature is to God as Child, so is Art to Nature

Nature is the art of God ~ Benjamin Disraeli

a maple leaf
broad yellow red
reaching out from where
it fell to autumn soil
so perfect   so complete
I cannot replicate
its beauty but simply seek
words that hide in shadows
until winter clears a path

Martin Shone

Martin lives in the Midlands, UK. He writes poetry and the occasional short story. He's also written a short novel for children about bullying and chess. He enjoys being around nature and is never without his notepad and pen.

He has self-published three books. *Silence Happens* and *Being Human* include his poetic thoughts about life, nature, peace, freedom and love, one example being, '*If a butterfly can change the weather, then our smiles can change the world*'. His third book, *After the Rain*, features over 100 of his poems.

There are links to his poetry and stories on his website: https://silencehappens.wordpress.com/

A Moment of Snowfall

How the clouds roil the sky's calm
with their droplets of chaos.
See how they tumble,
how they swirl,
how they create substance from separation,
how they join the dots once more,
only to lose them,
to watch them fall
into the arms of Gaia's embrace.
A white opera performed in silence
waiting for the crunch of applause.

Sharp Echoes

Sharp echoes of crows
tumble through the trees
scratching green paint off the leaves
to reveal autumn's gold.

Sunrise

Sunrise toasts the petals
into something beautiful
bringing to life
the fragrance of creation.

Ina Schroders-Zeeders

Ina was born in 1958 on the beautiful island of Terschelling in the Netherlands, where she still lives. She was widowed in 2016 and has three sons and two granddaughters.

Her poetry books in English are published by Winter Goose Publishing and include *Veritas*, *Amor*, *Roads book 1* and *Roads book 2*. She has also been published in poetry magazines and anthologies.

She is the author of a poetry book in Dutch, *Op weg naar het einde,* and has been writing novels for a Dutch publishing company for almost 20 years. She blogs at inaweblogisback.wordpress.com

The Balance

She weighs the thought by the weight of her child
As she carries him up the stairs –
The boy seems lighter –
But she won't speak of this with the father.

Slowly she reaches the landing,
Where she forces her thought over the balcony
It would crash the bed of the little one,
It would shake the house on its base,
And the walls would tumble down.

Lauren Scott

Lauren lives in the San Francisco Bay Area with her husband and chocolate Labrador, Copper, and she has two adult children. Her family is the joy of her life, but her passion is to write. Currently, she is working on a memoir, while simultaneously challenging herself by writing her first novel.

Writing poetry began in Lauren's youth, and she is inspired by all facets of life – its joys and its trials. She has published two poetry collections: *New Day, New Dreams* (2013) and *Finding a Balance* (2015). These two compilations explore romance, life's struggles, humour and moving forward.

By sharing her poetry, Lauren's wish is to delve into the emotions of her readers, hoping that her words resonate on some level with them.

Her poetry and book information can be found on her blog, Baydreamer: https://baydreamerbubble.com

One Kiss

I stare at this empty page,
white as the blanketed ground
in winter's staging

Where are the syllables I crave
to create a mixture of magic?
I fear they have travelled
to faraway places,
across desert dunes
and boundless oceans,

and might not return
so that I may tell him (again)
how he's irreplaceable

Instead,
I'll just kiss him
and steady myself
in the arms of a man
who is satisfied
with my
simple existence.

Katharine Towers

Katharine lives in the Peak District in the UK and has published two poetry collections, both with Picador. *The Floating Man* (2010) won the Seamus Heaney Centre Prize and was shortlisted for the Ted Hughes Award and the Aldeburgh First Collection Prize. Her latest collection, *The Remedies* (2016), was shortlisted for the TS Eliot Prize.

Katharine studied Modern Languages at St. Hilda's College Oxford and in 2007 completed an MA in Poetry at Newcastle University. She currently works as assistant editor at independent poetry publisher Candlestick Press. She also teaches poetry, running Poetry Surgeries for the Poetry Society and workshops at festivals and for universities. Katharine is currently Poet in Residence at the Cloud Appreciation Society.

www.katharinetowers.com

Double Concerto

For PB

Seeing your hand under his light arm
makes me think of Bach's two violins.

On the stairs you say you are too sad for music,
but there's a concert hush

as you steer him forward to the garden seat.
This is Bach: one violin takes up the tune,

makes us believe it's everything essential –
spirit, truth – then lets it lapse

so the other violin can know it too.
This is how it is: the tilt and sway

of melodies you share like oxygen,
breathing out, breathing in.

From *The Floating Man,* Picador (2010)

The Window

Standing at the window staring out
at no-one or at nothing was my mother,
anxious for a home-coming.
I hurried home all night, until I woke.
She stayed with me that morning,
silent as a child who's sad or cold,
then dwindled like a hope until
by evening she had died again.
All night I stood beside my window
catching cold and staring out
at nothing or at no-one coming home.

From *The Remedies*, Picador (2016)

The Way We Go

the way we go about our lives
trying out each empty room
like houses we might own
eavesdropping for clues in corridors until

standing at a gate or attic window
seeing beauty in a flag of sky
we're gone, leaving the doors open
all the lights burning

From *The Floating Man*, Picador (2010)

Rob Walton

Rob is a writer, performer and teacher from Scunthorpe in the UK. He now lives with his family in North Shields, from where he travels to perform in schools and libraries.

He once dressed as a silver-suited alien to promote a soft drink in a shopping centre, but wishes he hadn't mentioned it. His poems, short stories, nonsense and flash fictions for adults have appeared in various publications, including, most importantly, Scunthorpe United's matchday magazine.

Rob has written a number of books, articles and resources for teachers and has taught across the primary age range. His poems for children appear in The Emma Press anthology, *Watcher of the Skies, Poems about Space and Aliens*, Frances Lincoln's *Let's Play!* (poems about sports and games from around the world) and *Dear Tomato* (food and agriculture poems).

He collated the text for the New Memorial Pathway to commemorate the 150th anniversary of the Hartley Pit Disaster, and was winner of the National Flash Fiction Day micro-fiction competition 2015. Rob's poem for children 'Letters' featured on the 2016 National Poetry Day website. He has written and performed for many years with The Big Fun Club.

An Alien Complains

Which one of you Earthers
Decided to portray us
As purple and green
And walking around naked?

We come in the full range
Of colours, tones and shades,
And the majority – the *vast* majority –
Of us wear smart and fashionable clothes.
Some of us have contracts
To wear designer labels.
There are also those who hate
The whole label thing,
Yet are still smarter
Than *you*.

It seems to me
You've been trying to stereotype us
Since you published those
Technicolour comics
And made those films
In the 1950s.
You should look at yourselves
Through 3-D glasses.

So few of us have tentacles
It's hardly worth mentioning

~148~

Yet you always go on about it.

Finally, there is only one person in my family
With three eyes
On either side of her head.
And that was a lifestyle choice.

The Thing About the Words

They want to be heard
They want to be read
They want to be tucked
Up in your bed
(They want to be *enveloped* by your duvet)

They want to run
They want to jump
They want to describe
The camel's hump
(They want to point out the difference between
          Bactrian and *dromedary*)

They want to reveal
They want to hide
They'll take pleasure
They'll take pride
(But they'll not be *big bad boasty beasties*)

They want to squash
They want to stretch
They want to carry
They want to fetch
(They want to bring the thesaurus from the long,
          extended, elongated, lengthy shelf)

And,

In my experience,
The words want to be written.

Maureen Weldon

Maureen, a former professional ballet dancer, is Irish and now lives in Wales in the UK. She has been writing for over thirty years and has been widely published nationally and internationally. Her poems have appeared in *Poetry Scotland*, *Ink Sweat & Tears*, *Crannóg* magazine, and *Vsesvit*, a Ukrainian journal, and she has won various awards.

In 2014, she represented Wales at the International festival, Terra Poetia. In 2011, she won The Sons of Camus International Journal New Feature Award. Her poem, 'He Tells Her' (see below), was Highly Commended in the SWWJ Elizabeth Longford Trophy Poetry Competition 2006.

Maureen enjoys giving readings, especially when accompanied by live music.

Her latest pamphlet, *Midnight Robin*, was published in 2014 by Poetry Space Ltd.

Midnight Robin

While the sky shimmers like shot silk,
chimneypots a toothy smile,
I count the pots, 1 2 3 4 5.

On my kitchen table, sheets and sheets
of screwed up poems,
I will flatten them tomorrow
for shopping lists.

While perfumed smells of hyacinths
bring memories of my mother:
'they make lovely Christmas presents'
she would say, as she potted and tended.

The evening moves along
as evenings do …
The moon a half golden bracelet.
The sky cluttered with stars.

All is still, no trains, no cars.
And in this stillness
the midnight robin sings.

First published in Crannóg *magazine.*

He Tells Her

She lives her life
in boxes,
or signed
on the bottom line.

The in-laws,
the rotten husband,
and jam making.

And the child –
that joy – the child.

Then grandmother,
rather wild, chilled out,
good at making pastry.

And friends, they are the ones,
do not forget,
they will remind you of
what you have forgotten.

So, maybe tomorrow
is the day to stand
by the edge of the water …

As the tide turns,
where the past sucks secrets
through a shell.

*Highly Commended, SWWJ Elizabeth Longford Trophy Poetry
Competition 2006.*

The Past

I have left the past,
or so I thought;
yet it sits in every corner,
sits on my back.

Sometimes the long garden with a hammock
to swing in, to laze in,
near the sweet peas, near the roses.

Sometimes a white breeze
salty from the ocean.

It is Ireland, England, Scotland, Wales.

It is war-time, it is peace-time.

It is a wedding vow torn by the wind.

It is sitting around a table, laughing.

It is the dearest dead.

It is christening the baby.

It is like a cave,
or a pass through the mountain.

And always the still small voice.

First published in The Passionate Transitory *e-zine.*

Frederick E. Whitehead

Frederick lives about 40 minutes south of Buffalo New York in the United States.

He is the author of eight volumes of poetry. His latest, *Bewilderhof*, came out in early 2017. He hosts a monthly Poetry Series at Dog Ears Bookstore & Café, South Buffalo, and blogs at fewhitehead.wordpress.com.

Frederick also publishes limited run chapbooks through his Destitute Press. His books can be found online at various bookseller sites.

Grind

the crank on the street organ
needs grease
but the only one it seems to bother
      is the monkey

he is stomping his miniature fez
out of frustration
as the elderly
return coins to their pockets

customer service
it seems
disgusts
them more and more lately

every seventh note is a metallic squeak
      the grinder grinds away
no closer to the rent
than he was this morning

the monkey just stripped off his
vest and is pissing in the potted
petunias over at the sidewalk cafe

I'm too tired to try to understand it all
too tired to wrap it all up
into a tidy metaphor for our

collective insanity
so I turn in to the closest tavern I see

it's nice
just me and the barkeep
a gentleman's agreement
to not speak

and the monkey
glowering
over his little tin cup of beer

Steerage

there are those days
when, 20 min. in you begin
to believe the evidence
that suggests a mistake, but

the ship has already left the slip
with you on it
      so, there it is

maybe along the way
some stratification will occur
heavier emotion
settling out across the seabed
of your day

the current of all the rest
swirling above
barely keeping
the rusting bulk afloat

down in steerage
      pressed against the throng
you have only
fresh air and solitude
on your mind

as the ship
quite unapologetically
steams ahead

Sarah Whiteley

Sarah Whiteley is a Seattle poet with Midwestern roots. She is the author of *No Direction But Home* (ALL CAPS Publishing, 2013), which explores some of her favourite themes: travel, nature, and finding home.

She is hard at work on her next chapbook and currently writes at ebbtide.wordpress.com

Ciphers

this morning there is an arrangement of house finches
scattering ciphers of seed on the window sill,
with one grey-capped junco for cheeky emphasis

I've tried yet again, but cannot seem to read
these classified messages they leave,
but imagine them something bright and flippant

At Talapus

that day at Talapus

the jays played
in the pines above,

gracing our fingers
with intrepid feet

– strikingly light
and agile things –

like briefly holding
a sliver of delight,

bright-eyed and fleeting,

as joyous things
tend to be

The Peony

I planted a peony
against the fence

— showy, extravagant —

a frivolous bloom
to cup the moon

but the afternoon
after that fierce rain

— dogged, relentless —

I found the flower
had been crushed

and the moon had dropped
her pearls in the grass

Jane Williams

Jane Williams is an Australian writer based in Tasmania. She is the author of five books of poems and a collection of stories.

While best known for her poetry, Jane enjoys writing across forms and genres and in collaboration with other artists. She has read her poetry in USA, Canada, Ireland, England, Malaysia, Czech Republic and Slovakia where she held a three month residency in 2016.

https://janewilliams.wordpress.com

I have Come to Believe

angels take the shape
of small industrious birds
permit them
to alight on your shoulders
fuss over any fallout
commit
to their ministrations
allow them infiltrate
your dreams
when you lose hope
trust them
to pick up the thread
each day bless them
ancient stitchers
of the shopworn
human heart

Sandy Wilson

Sandy started writing by contributing humorous and sometimes poignant stories to his daughter's blog about her childhood in Leeds, England, and his in Scotland.

To develop further as a writer, Sandy joined a creative writing group in Otley, West Yorkshire, UK, led by the Yorkshire poet James Morgan Nash. In his two years of membership he has written memoirs, fiction, flash fiction, and poetry.

His work has been published on the American website 'The Drabble' and included, alongside those of James Morgan Nash, Glenda Kerney Brown and Christine Moran, in the anthology, *The Pulse of Everything*. Sandy's memoir, *Memory Spill*, about his childhood in Scotland is available on Amazon.

He blogs at www.sandyscribbler.com

The Arc of Time

As the arc of time passes my given span
And turns relentlessly to the moment
Now I too must soon pay the ferryman.

Will I need a holy tome, a Bible or Koran,
Or a book of good deeds and sins I repent
As the arc of time passes my given span?

Will you meet me, your son, now a man
Recognise me, this time worn remnant
Now I too must soon pay the ferryman?

Will we talk of our life shared if you can
Before you were taken, your time spent
As the arc of time passes my given span?

Will you ask me how went my life's plan
Does my book of days tell of joy or lament
Now I too must soon pay the ferryman?

Will I tell you that life perdured as it began
Days of light, and shadow, without relent
As the arc of time passes my given span
Now I too must soon pay the ferryman.

The Caress of Spring

Spring arrives
the tantalising
slow caress
of a lover's hand
on my body
as I awake from
deep sleep
dark dreams.

Bart Wolffe

Bart died in 2016 while this anthology was being prepared. The poems included here were selected by him before his death.

After many years in the advertising industry in Zimbabwe, working with both electronic media and print, Bart developed as an independent writer and theatre practitioner responsible for running workshops throughout the countries of southern Africa. He worked with many organisations, including the Catholic Commission for Justice and Peace, the British Council, The Goethe Institute, and Alliance Française.

In 1997, Bart brought a team of actors to London and Edinburgh to perform six of his plays, and in June 2010, he ran eight workshops with refugee children from schools around Croydon in the UK.

His work has been widely recognised with both awards and positive reviews in many international publications. His portfolio, which includes plays, novels and poetry, reflects his passion for giving voice to the voiceless, minorities and dispossessed individuals.

After leaving Zimbabwe in 2003, Bart spent two years in Germany before settling in England.

The Boy Who Never Grew Up

Some said he was stranger than most. I suppose
Someone who picks up dead bones from their graves
In the tangled matted grass might be different.
But he liked the purity of those white sticks,
Their sculpted lines. He would trace
The fine cracks, the slender twigs of a bird's breast
Or a lizard's triangulated head. He placed these
In various corners of his world. An old tin
Or a rusted drum would become a repository
For fallen feathers. He also collected odd stones
For they spoke to him. Each one a character in a book
Only he could read. Sometimes it was an agate
Whose whorls reminded him of a cut stump
From that favourite fallen Musasa tree
And the thin rings that recorded drought years.
He preferred a piece of bark, lichen encrusted
To anything shining, new or plastic on the shelf.
Decay was real, was tangible. A patch of ground
Defied the bland horizon of a whitewashed school wall,
A seed pod, screwed and curled, its twisted shape
Was a vowel, a word, a world. A bit of rotting wood,
A snail shell, a thorn, a horn, a broken tooth;
Each icon had its roughness, edges for fingers to read
And unseen in his pocket, let him touch its solid fact.
Engrained like the fingerprints that were his alone
Deeper than anyone might have known beneath his skin
He knew the secrets of what mattered stayed hidden
For his eyes only, his fingers, his memory, his own truth.

Tinker, Tailor Soldier, Sailor

The rag-and-bone man is leading the procession
With his horse and cart, bus and cars following
In some funeral cortege to the death of time.
In no hurry for progress, he gathers rusted scraps
Of the expired. People bring out their dead
For him to load on the slow wagon of tradition.
An old stove, bits of lead piping, metal piled
Onto the wooden frame of his cross that he burdens
Each day from dawn to dusk, to his way's end.
His philosophy, gathered from his father's father:
"Where there's muck, there's brass ..."
The world that queues behind his clopping nag
May be impatient to move on, their schedules calling,
But the stars and moon turn at his pace, not theirs.
In passing, he tilts his cap towards me sitting watching,
His one-trick pony also nods as the steady gait
Of hooves and creaking wheels haul history,
Two travellers down the road of broken dreams.

Eclipse

Soundless and without warning the sky
Sucked in its breath. A shadowed hand
Of the demon darkened the light, swollen
As if announcing war over the nature of things.
Birds paused, mid-song, seeming uncertain
Of the change. The labourer in the field
Stopped hoeing, his bowed head lifted,
All so suddenly and terribly mute.
Trees became silhouettes and even stars looked on
Momentarily. The sun stood still. Swallowed
And defeated by the threat and superstition
Men dreamt black thoughts in the morning's middle
If only for a passing while
Before waking for the second time today.

~173~

The Book Bus

One in six adults around the world have come through childhood unable to read and write, due mainly to a lack of books and opportunity to read. The Book Bus was founded by publisher Tom Maschler with the aim of supplying books and making them accessible to children to help get more children reading and therefore be able to make more choices about their own lives.

In 2008 the Book Bus began delivering books to schools in Zambia and working with children to inspire them to read. The Book Bus has opened reading schemes in Zambia, Malawi, and Ecuador where over 100,000 children now have books that are relevant and accessible to read.

www.thebookbus.org

Bennison Books

Bennison Books has four imprints:

Contemporary Classics
Great writing from new authors

Non-Fiction
Interesting and useful works written by experts

People's Classics
Handpicked golden oldies by favourite and forgotten authors

Poetic Licence
Poetry and prosetry

Bennison Books is named after Ronald Bennison, an aptly named blessing.

Bennisonbooks.com

Printed in Great Britain
by Amazon